P9-DWU-288

# The Irish Setter

# A PET-CARE HANDBOOK

# The Irish Setter

Catherine G. Sutton

MCMLXXXII

South Group Ltd., Publishers

LEICESTER – NEW YORK

ISBN (UK) : 0 7118 0001 4
ISBN (USA) : 0 940 842 01 7

© MCMLXXXI
South Group (Leicester) Ltd., Publishers

*No part of this publication may be reproduced, stored in a
retrieval system, or transmitted, in any form or by any means,
electronic, mechanical, photocopying, recording, or otherwise
without the prior permission of the Publisher.*

# Contents

# Introduction

In this brief work on the Irish Setter I can only try to give you a general picture of this very delightful and glamorous gundog. His rich chestnut coat finds him very many admirers and once one has got to know this devil-may-care Irishman it is difficult to find a substitute for him or her.

He is quite excellent in the home with his family. He is a great show dog and many of this breed have gained top honours at home and abroad. He is equally remarkable in the field as a worker and has also distinguished himself as an efficient obedience worker. He is, therefore, as versatile as he is charming and with correct care and attention can settle to live happily in a flat just as he can in the squire's drawing room. He loves human companionship and will return in full measure his appreciation of a happy home amongst friends.

In choosing the Irish Setter you have chosen a dog that needs regular grooming to keep his coat in good condition. He also requires regular exercise to keep him happy, fit and well muscled and being a little headstrong on occasions he must have strict discipline. Give him all these things plus his correct food and you will have found yourself a devoted companion opening up many doors of pleasure and excitement for you. He will reward you with loyalty and affection. The onus is entirely yours.

I am writing this book mainly for the novice exhibitor or breeder and for those who are buying or thinking of buying their first Irish Setter. It could well be that from these people will come the breeders and exhibitors of the future. If I have helped in any way to start someone off on the right foot and perhaps even encourage another to come into the breed then I feel that this little book will have merited its existence.

# History of the Irish Setter

A true 'Irishman' in so many ways. He can be stubborn and wilful on one occasion and yet on another he can be so charming with his happy-go-lucky manner and his rollicking gay nature. That his past is shrouded in mystery can be readily understood when one realises that he essentially comes from and belongs to Ireland. I am sure that it is his typically Irish character that endears him to so many.

He was known as the Red Spaniel in the early part of the last Century. In Gaelic they were called Modder Rhu which translated means the Red Dog. The Irish have always been renowned for their great love of sport and it is therefore not surprising to learn that the Irish Setter was recognised as the King of Sporting Dogs to these sporting enthusiasts. In Ireland he had a reputation second to none for winning the Field Trials and now in modern times he still retains this reputation as a great bird dog.

It is certainly true to say that he has been pure bred for many a long day and breeders of other Setters have gone to him and relied on him to improve their Setters by using his bloodlines. In the last Century there seemed to be great controversy over the question of whether or not white should be allowed in the coat. Breeders argued about this at great length and some even believed that white markings were essential and positive proof of purity in the breed.

In 1874 at the Dublin Show special classes were scheduled for Red and Red-and-White Setters. It was after that show that the Ulster Irish Setter Club decided that the breed should be known in future as the Irish Setter and this remains today. In England the first dog show for Pointers and Setters was held in 1859 and in 1865 the first Field Trial was organised.

Progress continued to be made both in the show ring and at Field Trials, but it was not until about 1920 that they really got what they considered in those days to be large entries although today they would be infinitesimal in comparison.

With the advent of World War II things slowed down again and all activities in the breed had to be severely curtailed.

Just when things were getting going again after the war a very serious disease reared its ugly head in the breed and 1946 was a disaster year for the Irish Setter. This disease which is now known as Progressive Retinal Atrophy was in those days known simply as 'night blindness'. This was proved to be hereditary and steps had to be taken to trace back to the guilty party. With the help of Mr. W. J. Rasbridge, a very knowledgeable student of genetics, plus the co-operation of the Kennel Club, the breeders, often at great cost to themselves, wholeheartedly set out to try and eradicate this scourge.

The first symptoms of this disease seemed to be the inability of the dog to see in a failing light. As this progressed the symptoms became much worse and the dog found it difficult to see even in good daylight. Eventually the dog became blind and think of the sadness that this alone must have brought to his breeder and owner. To trace back to the real offender who started it all was a very difficult task because so often it was found that dogs were carriers of the disease but showed no symptoms themselves.

The breeders were dedicated to their job of trying to put a stop to this disease. No secret was made of this affliction and all breeders were made well aware of what to look for and what to expect in dogs that were unfortunate enough to be victims. It was a very great credit to those breeders that the disease was in time almost completely eradicated. This was not without terrible heartaches and sadness and the awful worry of running on litters to discover whether or not they were free from P.R.A., to say nothing of the incalculable expense. Because of their loyalty and devotion to their breed the breeders of these troublesome days richly deserve the success that the Irish Setter now enjoys not only in this country but in many other lands overseas.

Today the Irish Setter is very firmly established as one of our top Gundogs and at the end of 1980 had close to 6,000 registrations at the English Kennel Club.

As far as the history of the Irish Setter in the USA is concerned I like to quote Mrs. Luz Holderstot. She says:
'In the 1870's two noted Red Setters were sent to America.

*Published in 1800 The Cynographia Britannica by Sydenham Edwards contained this illustration of early Setters. The Irish is in the centre with the English in foreground and Scottish in background.*

Elcho arrived at the age of about one year in 1875. Elcho was bought by Charles H. Turner of St. Louis, Missouri, who had plenty of money and leisure time, and who wanted the finest dog possible. Elcho had appeared at the Dublin Dog Show, being shown for his breeder and then-owner, Mr. Oppenheimer of St. Petersburg, Russia, by Robert S. Greenhill.

When Elcho arrived in this country, there was a tremendous interest in him, as purebred dogs were at that time a rarity here. As a consequence, he was practically unbeatable in the show rings. Indeed, he was a most attractive dog, being well-proportioned, smooth of shoulders, with depth of chest, possessing a pretty head with well defined stop, and welldeveloped, muscular quarters and good angulation. Due to Elcho's poorer showing in the field, Mr. Turner, after producing several sons from him, sold him to Dr. William Jarvis of Claremont, New Hampshire. This doctor was one of the pioneers of Irish Setter breeding in this country. Among Elcho's famous offspring was his son, Elcho Jr. out of Noreen, who traced back to the great Palmerston, sire of Garryowen. Elcho Jr.'s picture shows a substantial dog of balanced proportions, a well-defined-stop, smooth, flat coat, with light feathering.

From the time of Elcho's prominence in American show rings up to 1900, the Irish Setter gained fame mainly through success in the show ring. From 1874 to 1948, a period of 74 years, 375 dogs sired approximately 760 bench show champions. Of these, only five were field trial champions. The general cause was that the field dogs were not trained nor conditioned for the show ring, and their owners were interested in field performance rather than 'beauty contests.'

In spite of the growing success of this breed in the show ring, it must not be assumed that the Irish Setter was not to be found in field trials. He was there, but in small numbers; therefore, his reputation as an outstanding field dog was not great.

In the late 1940's, several new strains were being developed by breeders mostly interested in show dogs. Their dogs were larger, more elegant, with longer faces and more and more spectacular coats. One of the most outstanding strains in the country was started by William W. Higgins of Caldwell, New Jersey.

Higgins' most famous foundation bitch was Craigie Lea Mona, a beautiful solid mahogany specimen who was thoroughly field broken. When bred to the outstanding English Champion, Higgins' Paddy of Boyne, this breeding produced a fine litter, possessing both 'type' and bird sense. The most noted of the litter was Higgins' Red Pat. At the age of four, he was Best of Breed at both Westminster and Morris and Essex shows. At the Fourth Annual Specialty show of the Irish Setter Club of America at Cornwell, N.Y. when Pat was six years old, he was awarded Best in Show. The second mating of the two produced Ch. Higgins' Red Coat. This dog was to become the progenitor of just about every Irish Setter in America. The best known son born to Red Coat, Ch. Milson O'Boy, is best remembered for his great win at the Morris and Essex show in 1935, which was held on the estate of Geraldine Dodge, and where he topped an entry of 3,000 dogs for Best in Show. He sired 17 champions, many to be found in the pedigrees of present day kennels.

A grandson of Red Coat's, Ch. Kinvarra Kermit, who died in 1948, was the sire of 21 litters, totaling 171 puppies, of which 28 became champions. Lee Schoen of Darian, Connecticut bought 'Kermit' as a puppy from Ted Eldridge.

Today, the Eldridge Kennels and their prefix, Tirvelda, located in Middleburg, Virginia are world famous, and the dogs from that kennel have somewhat changed the type seen in the ring. Many sincere and carefully-planned programs from such kennels as Lee Schoen's Kinvarra kennels, the Knightscroft Kennels of New City owned by Joe and Henrietta Knight, Crosshaven of California, Tyronne Farms at Tipton, Iowa owned by Jack Spear and the End O'Maine kennels of Hollis Wilson, fostered the rapid increase and interest in the breed from 1930 to 1941'.

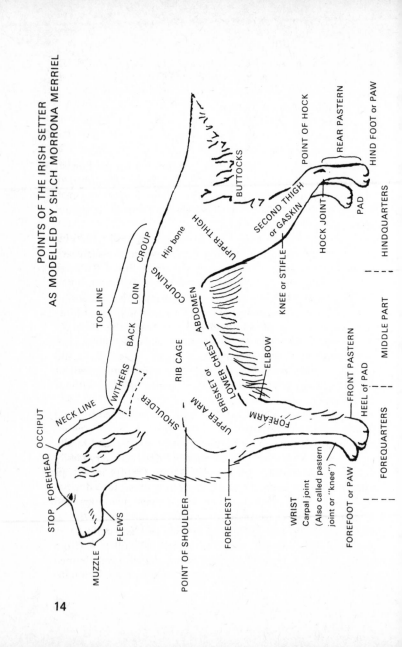

POINTS OF THE IRISH SETTER
AS MODELLED BY SH.CH MORRONA MERRIEL

MUZZLE
FLEWS
STOP
FOREHEAD
OCCIPUT
NECK LINE
WITHERS
TOP LINE
BACK
LOIN
CROUP
COUPLING
Hip bone
UPPER THIGH
BUTTOCKS
SECOND THIGH or GASKIN
POINT OF HOCK
REAR PASTERN
HIND FOOT or PAW
PAD
HOCK JOINT
KNEE or STIFLE
ABDOMEN
RIB CAGE
SHOULDER
UPPER ARM
BRISKET or LOWER CHEST
ELBOW
FOREARM
FRONT PASTERN
HEEL of PAD
POINT OF SHOULDER
FORECHEST
WRIST
Carpal joint
(Also called pastern
joint or "knee")
FOREFOOT or PAW

FOREQUARTERS
MIDDLE PART
HINDQUARTERS

14

# The Standard of the Irish Setter

The Standard of the Irish Setter is laid down by the English Kennel Club and this is the guide that all judges and breeders must try to follow. Quite obviously everyone does not read the Standard with quite the same eye but overall it should produce a very similar picture.

The Irish Red Setter Club was formed in Dublin in 1885 by several Irish Setter enthusiasts many of whom were lawyers. In 1886 the produced a Standard for the Irish Setter. This was on a points system, i.e. so many points for head, eyes, body, legs, etc., and when our Kennel Club assumed the responsibility for the Standards of all breeds that came under their jurisdiction, and this included Northern Ireland, the Scale of Points was done away with altogether. This, of course, was done with the full co-operation of all the Breed Clubs and obviously took time to prepare and to come to an agreement on. Any alteration to this Standard cannot be done without the approval of the Kennel Club.

Let us now look at this Standard which is published by kind permission of the Kennel Club.

**General appearance** Must be racy, full of quality, and kindly in expression. (From this description one can very easily visualise a good picture of the Irish Setter. Quality is perhaps a little difficult to describe but to me it means that a dog has that little extra something which puts it above the normal and almost transforms a good dog to an even better dog).

**Head and skull** The head should be long and lean, not narrow or snipy, and not coarse at the ears. The skull oval (from ear to ear) having plenty of brain room, and with well-defined occipital protuberance. Brows raised, showing stop. The muzzle moderately deep, and fairly square at the end. From the stop to the point of the nose should be long, the nostrils wide, and the jaws of nearly equal length, flews not to be pendulous. The colour of the nose: dark mahogany, or dark walnut, or black. (The occiput is the rear of the skull and the Standard requires that it should have a well-defined prominence. Stop is the depression between the eyes at the junction of skull and nose. Flews not to be pendulous which means that they should not hang down over the mouth as in a Bloodhound).

**Eyes** Should be dark hazel or dark brown and ought not to be too large. (This description is quite clear and in my opinion too large an eye takes away from the very necessary kind expression of the Setter).

**Ears** The ears should be of moderate size, fine in texture, set on low, well back; hanging in a neat fold close to the head.

**Mouth** Not over or undershot. (I feel that this could be more clearly defined particularly for the novice. Obviously this means that the mouth should be level or even and to those more knowledgeable this conveys that it should be a scissor bite. In this case the upper incisor teeth should very slightly project beyond the lower teeth, fitting very tightly like scissors. I would also like to add here that the teeth should be strong, large and sound).

**Neck** Should be moderately long, very muscular, not not too thick, slightly arched, free from all tendency to throatiness.

**Forequarters** The shoulders to be fine at the points, deep and sloping well back. The chest as deep as possible, rather narrow in front. The forelegs should be straight and sinewy, having plenty of bone, with elbows free, well let down, not inclined either in or out. (Unless one has a shoulder that slopes well back it is not possible to get the desired length of neck. If the Irish Setter has an upright shoulder in which the scapula starts at the shoulder but goes down almost perpendicularly, he would be greatly restricted in his movement both in speed and scope and he would be susceptible to great jarring through those upright shoulders. Loaded shoulders, i.e. heavy bulky shoulders, are most undesirable and it is up to owners not to allow any superfluous fat or muscle padding on the shoulders. Once there, it is extremely difficult to get rid of and the animal will lose that lovely streamlined outline so characteristic of the breed).

**Body** Should be proportionate, the ribs well sprung, leaving plenty of lung room. Loins muscular, slightly arched. (Well sprung ribs are essential to provide, primarily, adequate lung space and heart room and with this should go a good depth of chest).

**Hindquarters** Should be wide and powerful. The hind legs from hip to hock should be long and muscular; from hock to heel short and strong. The stifle and hock joints well bent, and not inclined either in or out. (As the quarters play an important part in the dog's movement it is essential that the quarters should be powerful in order to have enough propelling force to drive the dog along. This is very dependent upon the muscular power which has developed in the second thigh. I quote from Smythe in the *Conformation of the Dog*— 'Practically the whole propelling force of the hind limb is dependent on the ability of the dog to straighten the leg from the state of angulation to complete extension, as forcibly and rapidly as may be required. This is dependent entirely upon the muscle power of a well-developed second thigh'. To get this correct development and muscular condition regular free exercise is essential plus controlled road exercise).

**Feet** Should be small, very firm, toes strong, close together and arched.

**Tail** Should be of moderate length, proportionate to the size of the body, set on rather low, strong at root, and tapering to a fine point; to be carried as nearly as possible on a level with or below the back. (The tail finishes the picture of the Irish Setter and is an extension of the spinal column. A tail that comes up over the back like a hound or curls at the end should be heavily penalised and is foreign to the breed although sometimes seen! The tail feathering should hang in

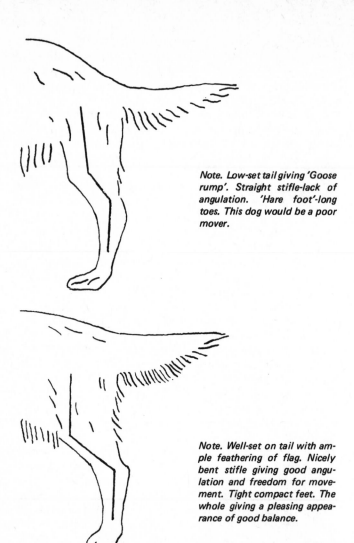

*Note. Low-set tail giving 'Goose rump'. Straight stifle-lack of angulation. 'Hare foot'-long toes. This dog would be a poor mover.*

*Note. Well-set on tail with ample feathering of flag. Nicely bent stifle giving good angulation and freedom for movement. Tight compact feet. The whole giving a pleasing appearance of good balance.*

*Good front. Straight legs, good bone, tight feet, turned neither out or in. Elbows well tucked in.*

*Bad front. Bowed legs, toes out-if toes turned straight elbows would probably turn out. Front to wide.*

*Good rear. Note hocks neither turned in or out with result that feet are correctly placed.*

*Bad rear. Cow-hocked thus throwing feet out-this dog would move very badly.*

long fringes with the length of the fringes increasing from a little beyond the set-on of the tail to the middle of the tail and then gradually decreasing to the end of the tail).

**Coat and Feathering** On the head, front of the legs, and tips of the ears, should be short and fine, but on all other parts of the body and legs it ought to be of moderate length, flat and as free as possible from curl or wave. The feather on the upper portion of the ears should be long and silky; on the back of fore and hind legs should be long and fine; a fair amount of hair on the belly, forming a nice fringe, which may extend on chest and throat. Feet to be well feathered between the toes. Tail to have a nice fringe or moderately long hair, decreasing in length as it approaches the point. All feathering to be as straight and as flat as possible.

**Colour** The colour should be rich chestnut, with no trace whatever of black; white on chest, throat or toes, or a small star on the forehead, or a narrow streak or blaze on the nose or face not to disqualify.

**Note** Male animals should have two apparently normal testicles fully descended into the scrotum.

The above is the Standard as laid down by the Kennel Club and it may be surprising to some to note that there is no restriction as to height or weight laid down in this Standard. This is obviously accepted by the breeders but I personally feel that even a guiding line would be beneficial and give newcomers some idea of the approximate size to aim for in their breeding programme.

The American Standard does, in fact, fill in this gap and varies slightly from our own Standard. By kind permission of the American Kennel Club I reproduce it herewith.

### AMERICAN KENNEL CLUB OFFICIAL
### STANDARD FOR THE IRISH SETTER

**General appearance** The Irish Setter is an active, aristocratic bird-dog, rich red in color, substantial yet elegant in build.

Standing over two feet tall at the shoulder, the dog has a straight, fine, glossy coat, longer on ears, chest, tail, and back legs. Afield he is a swift-moving hunter; at home, a sweet-natured, trainable companion. His is a rollicking personality.

**Head** Long and lean, its length at least double the width between the ears. The brow is raised, showing a distinct stop midway between the tip of nose and the well-defined occiput (rear point of skull). Thus the nearly level line from occiput to brow is set a little above, and parallel to, the straight and equal line from eye to nose. The skull is oval when viewed from above or front; very slightly domed when viewed in profile. Beauty of head is emphasized by delicate chiseling along the muzzle, around and below the eyes, and along the cheeks. Muzzle moderately deep, nostrils wide, jaws of nearly equal length. Upper lips fairly square but not pendulous, the underline of the jaws being almost parallel with the top line of the muzzle. The teeth meet in a scissors bite in which the upper incisors fit closely over the lower, or they may meet evenly.

**Nose** Black or chocolate.

**Eyes** Somewhat almond-shaped, of medium size, placed rather well apart; neither deep-set nor bulging. Color, dark to medium brown. Expression soft yet alert.

**Ears** Set well back and low, not above level of eye. Leather thin, hanging in a neat fold close to the head, and nearly long enough to reach the nose.

**Neck** Moderately long, strong but not thick, and slightly arched; free from throatiness and fitting smoothly into the shoulders.

**Body** Sufficiently long to permit a straight and free stride. Shoulder blades long, wide, sloping well back, fairly close together at the top, and joined in front to long upper arms angled to bring the elbows slightly rearward along the brisket. Chest deep, reaching approximately to the elbows; rather narrow in front. Ribs well sprung. Loins of moderate length, muscular and slightly arched. Top line of body from withers to tail slopes slightly downward without sharp drop at the croup.

*U.S.A. Champion Danalee Bright Legend.*

*U.S.A. Champion Webline Fame'N'Fortune.*

Hindquarters should be wide and powerful with broad, well-developed thights.

**Legs and Feet** All legs sturdy, with plenty of bone, and strong, nearly straight pastern. Feet rather small, very firm, toes arched and close. Forelegs straight and sinewy, the elbows moving freely. Hind legs long and muscular from hip to hock, short and nearly perpendicular from hock to ground; well angulated at stifle and hock joints, which, like the elbows, incline neither in nor out.

**Tail** Strong at root, tapering to fine point, about long enough to reach the hock. Carriage straight or curving slightly upward, nearly level with the back.

**Coat** Short and fine on head, forelegs, and tips of ears; on all other parts, of moderate length and flat. Feathering long and silky on ears; on back of forelegs and thighs long and fine, with a pleasing fringe of hair on belly and brisket extending on to the chest. Feet well feathered between the toes. Fringe on tail moderately long and tapering. All coat and feathering as straight and free as possible from curl or wave.

**Color** Mahogany or rich chestnut red, with no trace of black. A small amount of white on chest, throat, or toes, or a narrow centered streak on skull, is not to be penalized.

**Size** There is no disqualification as to size. The make and fit of all parts and their over-all balance in the animal are rated more important. Twenty-seven inches at the withers and a show weight of about 70 pounds is considered ideal for a dog; the bitch 25 inches, 60 pounds. Variance beyond an inch up or down to be discouraged.

**Gait** At the trot the gait is big, very lively, graceful and efficient. The head is held high. The hindquarters drive smoothly and with great power. The forleges reach well ahead as if to pull in the ground, without giving the appearance of a hackney gait. The dog runs as he stands; straight. Seen from the front or rear, the forelegs, as well as the hind legs below the hock joint, move perpendicularly to the ground, with some tendency toward a single track as speed increases. But a crossing or

*U.S.A. Champion Tirvelda Red Baron of Dunholm.*

weaving of the legs, front or back, is objectionable.

**Balance** At his best, the lines of the Irish Setter so satisfy in over-all balance that artists have termed him the most beautiful of all dogs. The correct specimen always exhibits balance whether standing or in motion. Each part of the dog flows and fits smoothly into its neighbouring parts without calling attention to itself.

# Buying your Puppy

You really have decided to buy an Irish Setter puppy? You have thought about it very carefully. You have decided that when it is fully grown that it will not be too big for your home and your family? You have realised that it will take a good part of your free time for exercising, grooming and generally looking after it? The Irish Setter does not eat a tremendous amount of food when it is fully mature but to get it to that stage there must be no expense spared in its rearing. (See diet).

You may have seen one of your neighbours with one of the glamour boys or girls of this breed and just thought it would be nice to have one too. Do think about it more carefully than that as there is lot more to it than that. Don't please think that I am trying to put you off owning an Irish Setter. This is furthest from my mind but I do just want you to guard against possessing something that you may not be able to care for properly in one way or another and then there has to be a very sad parting. This is not only sad for you but for the dog concerned and everything must be done to try to avoid such a happening and this really lies in your hands.

In purchasing a puppy quite obviously the best place to go is where he was bred, i.e. the breeder. The names of reliable breeders can be supplied by the Kennel Club, at 1 Clarges Street, Piccadilly, London W.1. or found in either of the two weekly Dog Papers, *Our Dogs*, Oxford Road Station Approach, Manchester, or *Dog World*, 32, New Street, Ashford, Kent. Any good newsagent will supply these papers on request. Another good idea is to go along to one of your local dog shows. Information about these can be found in the Dog

Papers. At these shows you will find enthusiasts of the breed and they, will be only too happy to discuss the breed with you. The more you can learn about the Irish Setter before you actually become an owner the better for both you and the dog.

If you really want to see Irish Setters in full bloom I would suggest that you venture even further and visit one of the Championship Shows, either a General Championship Show or a Breed Championship Show. In this present year you will be likely to see anything from 200 to 300 Irish Setters being exhibited by the top breeders in the country. What better place to educate yourself about the Setter and his habits than from the most knowledgeable breeders.

It is always a good thing to visit one or two kennels before you make your final decision. Please always do this by appointment as kennel owners are very busy people and so often harrassed by visitors who arrive without an appointment. Make an appointment and you will be most welcome and given

*Four healthy young Irish Setters amuse themselves with a mop head. (Photo: Peter Diment)*

the opportunity to see what the kennel owner has for sale be it as a pet puppy, a brood bitch or a future show prospect. The kennel owner will ask you not to touch the puppies and this is a very sensible precaution particularly if the puppies are not old enough to have been inoculated. Do not take umbrage about this no matter how much you want to pick up the youngsters and cuddle them. The kennel owner is only protecting his interests as think how disastrous it would be if because of a little carelessness a virus infection hit the kennels. It is no good being careful afterwards and you may consider it over protective but no breeder can afford to lose young stock and years of breeding through any stupidity on their part.

Once you have chosen your puppy, of course, it will be quite all right for you to pick it up and not only fondle it but look over it very carefully to make sure, as far as you can see, that it is healthy and fit.

Your new puppy should have bright eyes, alert and happy with no nasty discharge. His nose should be clean and healthy looking. Just open his mouth a little to make sure that his teeth are clear and white and that his gums are a healthy pink. His breath should not be sour of unpleasant but, of course this can depend on what he has been chewing a few minutes before! His coat, which will be short at this stage, should look bright and healthy and there should be no signs of irritation or scratching. If you are at all worried there is no harm done in asking the kennel owner to provide a Veterinary Health Certificate but if you have gone to a reputable breeder it is very unlikely that you will be sold anything but a fit puppy. Start right so that you may continue right.

In the kennel you should be able to see the dam of the puppies and very probably the sire as well. You will know by the overall conditions of the kennel and how the inmates look if you have chosen the right sort of kennel to buy from and this is very important. You can hardly expect a sound, healthy puppy to come from a kennel where the general run of things

*An Irish Setter has a most gentle disposition and will make friends with any breed—especially his own relatives—the English Setter. (Photo: Peter Diment)*

does not appear to be quite right and where the older stock just does not look 100% in top condition. This can be a very good guide as to whether your puppy is coming from a good home or not. As to whether he is going to a good home is your responsibility.

Temperament is of paramount importance in your new puppy. When you first see the puppies there may be a little one—rather smaller than his brothers and sisters—that does not seem quite so forward nor quite so brave as the others. Often the smaller puppies are just as rough and cheeky as the bigger ones as they have had to stick up for themselves to survive. For those that are not quite so sure of themselves it often happens that when they are taken away from their brothers and sisters and have individual attention that they blossom out and forget all about their previous worries. However, if a puppy really seems frightened and tends to run back into his house be just a little wary of him unless you are prepared to give him that little bit of extra attention which he obviously wants and needs. If you can see his mother and father and test them for temperament—i.e. whether they will come to you happily or whether they tend to shy away—this can be a useful guide in assessing your puppy's temperament. If you are purchasing a show puppy the temperament must be good right from the word go and it would be unwise to consider anything that is not 100% good even as a baby.

Most breeders will not allow the puppies to leave for their new homes until they are at least eight to ten weeks old. At this age it is unlikely that they will be inoculated against the scourges of the canine world, i.e. distemper, hepatitis, leptospirosis. All puppies have a certain amount of immunity passed on to them by their mother but it is up to the new owner to protect the puppy when it leaves its old home.

Until your puppy can have the full course of injections for the above infections please keep it away from all other forms of livestock particularly dogs and do not ever put it down in the street or roadway at this stage. Never think that because you feel your puppy seems to be missing his brothers and sisters that it would be a good idea to invite a canine friend to come and see him. This is just where infection could be lurking. It is not much to ask that you safeguard your new companion for a week or two until your Veterinary Surgeon has declared it quite clear to lead a normal social life.

When your puppy leaves the home of its birth and all its litter companions it is a very bewildering time for it. Different hands feed it—there are different smells quite strange to the puppy—it has lost its own surrounds that it knew so well and it has lost the companionship of the other puppies. Be particularly patient and kind at this stage and you will soon be rewarded with your puppy responding to your treatment. The kennel owner should have given you a diet sheet and this you should stick to with great regularity. The puppy has enough to cope with in his new surroundings without having to have his diet changed. This could easily upset his tummy and cause him even more discomfort and worry. It may be that he will be a little sick and upset by his first car trip home. This is very understandable so go armed with a towel or newspaper and on the return home do not feed him until he has had time to let his tummy settle. A little water with glucose added should suffice until it is obvious that he has got over the car trip. He will soon come back with renewed energy and appeal.

The breeder will have told you about worming the puppy and this should have been done, probably twice, before leaving the kennels. It is unfortunately true that very few puppies are ever born free from worms so please do not think that because your puppy has worms that he has come from a kennel that is not quite 100% in their hygiene. If the puppy shows signs of still retaining these pests then consult the breeder or your Veterinary Surgeon who will soon advise on the correct treatment. If they linger they will tend to stop the puppy's proper growth. Symptoms include rather a nasty breath or a tendancy for the puppy to draw his bottom along the floor or sometimes just irritability and off colour a little.

In his early stages a pup requires long periods of sleep and rest. An Irish Setter has to grow into a big dog and when he is very young this sleep and rest is most important. Please do not let the children disturb him if he is resting. He would not be allowed to disturb the children during their rest. Bringing up a puppy with children can be a marvellous way of teaching discipline to both parties and it can also cement a true friendship between child and dog.

There are certain papers that should be handed over to a new owner when he takes delivery of his puppy. First there is the pedigree, second the Kennel Club Registration Form fully completed if the puppy is not already registered. If the puppy is registered then a fully completed Kennel Club Transfer

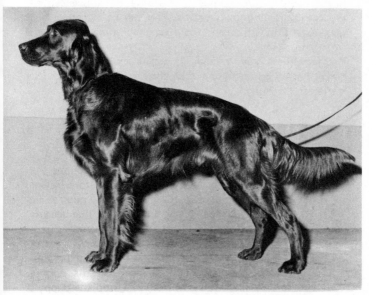

*Marrona Montero bred by Mrs. M. E. Stokes. (Photo: Diane Pearce)*

Form should be available. Not all puppies are registered by the breeder but the information should be available so that the new owner may do this. With the increased costs of breeding and maintaining a kennel a breeder may only decide to register what he considers show puppies. All the puppies in a litter cannot be beautiful ducklings. There must be the odd one or two ugly ducklings who may even have more character than their more glamorous brothers and sisters. These puppies will be just as sound and healthy and make perfect pets.

If you have purchased a bitch puppy with a view to breeding at a later date it is most important that you receive all the relevant documents so that her puppies can, in turn, be registered. If you have chosen a dog there is little point in registering him with the Kennel Club except, of course, it may please you to know that his name is on the official register.

In this country all dogs must have a Government licence from the age of six months onwards. This can be obtained from your local Post Office and the price at the time of writing is fifty pence.

You now have your puppy, its papers and a new responsibility. Let us go on to the next chapter and think about its rearing and training.

*Stand well clear, I'm coming out.*

*Irish Setters love exercise and are at their best when supplied with good opportunities for frequent exercise.*

*An Irish Setter photographed beautifully at the chase.*

*Resting after the retrieve.*

*This Irish Setter enjoys a swim.*

# Housing, rearing and training your puppy

In rearing and training your Setter puppy the first essential is always to remember to be kind but quite firm and to have great patience in the early stages of his life. This will all be rewarded in his later life when he will settle down as a well behaved member of your household and one that you can be proud to own.

**Housing** The small breeder or the household that has bought their Irish Setter as a companion or pet will no doubt bring the dog up in their own home. If it is decided that the Irish Setter should live outside at night or during the day please make quite sure that the shed or building is draught free and that he has a comfortable bed therein which stands on legs off the floor. Brick buildings with concrete floors are better than wooden buildings with wooden floors as quite obviously the former are easier to keep clean by hosing down whereas the wooden building and floor rot quicker and retain the smell of urine. If your Setter is to be outside then try to give him a fenced run round his house so that he can come and go as he pleases. You will find that under these circumstances he will soon learn to keep his house clean if he has access to an outside run.

In an out-building it will be necessary to have some form of heating and lighting and let me say, straight away, that never, never, should oil lamps or paraffin stoves be used for lighting or heating. They spell destruction as it is so easy for accidents to happen with tragic results. I have found that electricity is by far the best but please remember to safeguard your dog from the leads that he might find attractive to chew and again with very unpleasant results. This can also apply to his quarters in your home so be warned at the outset.

In deciding upon the position of your Setter's kennel outside it is well to remember that you may have to make visits to his kennel at all sorts of hours during the day and night in cases of sickness and even perhaps whelping at a later stage. With this in mind it is wise to have his or her kennel as near your home as possible. It is not fun to have to attend to your dog during a cold blustery night if you have to trek miles down the garden. It will seem miles in the middle of the night under bad conditions even if it only 50 yards.

Whether your Setter is to live in the house with you or outside in his own kennel always make sure that his bed is big enough for him to stretch out on. He does not always want to lie like this but he must be able to do so when he feels like it. If he is in the house he should have his own blankets which must be washed regularly. If he is outside again he could have his own blankets or sacks. Some kennel owners prefer straw but I always think that with long coated dogs this is apt to

*Two Irish Setters will enjoy each others company though they will be more costly to keep. (Photo: Peter Diment)*

*Hartsbourne Mattie in exhibition stance. Breeder Mrs. E. Walker.
(Photo: Diane Pearce)*

encourage and harbour such things as fleas. With puppies in kennels I use wood wool which they love to snuffle through and apart from giving them fun it is clean and free from bugs. They look cosy in it and, of course, it is easily replaced but quite a bit more expensive than straw.

Wherever your Setter is housed he must always have easy access to fresh water at all times—this is most important.

If you are starting a kennel and wish to run two Setters, or maybe more, together in a large outside kennel and run try to arrange for a bench to be put in the run. This bench should be about four or five inches off the ground and big enough to comfortably take two Setters. The dogs will soon learn that these benches are more comfortable to lie on than the damp grass or concrete and lovely to sunbathe on in the summer.

Als these small points help to keep your Setter healthy and

happy and this must be your intention night from the beginning.

**Feeding** This is all important as the correct growth of your dog depends upon it almost entirely. Never forget that the greater part of your Setter's growing takes place within the first eighteen months of his life and therefore it is absolutely essential that he is not deprived of his necessary foods during that time. He will never make up in later years what he has lost during the vital early months of his puppyhood and youth. If you have chosen a bitch and want to breed from her later on it is imperative that she has been properly reared so that she can give to her puppies the necessary good start in life and not produce weedy offspring.

For your own puppy the breeder should have given you a diet sheet and it is terribly important that you follow the instructions contained therein.

Most breeders have their own thoughts on feeding and have come to the best conclusions over many years of trial and error. These diet sheets will vary very little. In my opinion there is nothing to substitute a dog'a natural diet of raw meat with the addition of carbohydrates in either wholemeal bread or one of the many good dog biscuit meals on the market. It is necessary to incorporate vitamins into the diet and I give, as follows, what I believe to be a balanced diet for your Setter from eight weeks old onwards.

**8 weeks**

**8 a.m.** Half pint of warm milk made either into one of the human breakfast foods such as porridge or soaked into wholemeal bread. Beat an egg into this every other day and add a good teaspoonful of glucose.

**12 noon** 5 to 6 ounces of raw meat or tripe (this is rough tripe direct from the slaughter house and not the bleached variety in the butchers' shops). Add to this a good handful of terrier meal that has been soaked in good gravy, plus a teaspoonful of bone meal prepared for animal feeding. The meat can be slightly cooked if preferred.

**4. p.m.** Half a pint of milk or a little more if the puppy will take it plus a teaspoonful of glucose.

**8 p.m.** Same as noon but instead of bone meal add 1 teaspoonful of Cod Liver Oil.

Always remember that every puppy is an individual and you may find that the above is just a little too much for him but he should not need any more than the suggested quantities. Always guard against getting him too fat whilst he is still growing. If his body gets too heavy for his legs there can be serious consequences and normal growth will not be sustained and it is then that deformities can occur. His bone, at this stage, is soft and with too much weight to carry will become mis-shaped and once this happens it cannot be put right. This is bad rearing.

At about twelve weeks the number of meals should be reduced to three per day, i.e. two meat meals and one milk meal with the meat and biscuit being gradually increased. When he gets to six months his meals can be reduced to two per day incorporating his milk with one of his meat meals and from a year onwards one meal should satisfy him with perhaps a drink of milk at lunch time or before he goes to bed. As he grows older the terrier meal should be substituted for a good hound meal. A fully grown Irish Setter should have about 1½lbs of meat a day plus his biscuit meal.

Meal must always be soaked with boiling liquid and left to cool. It should not be fed sloppy to the animal but it is essential that it should have swollen to its fullest extent otherwise it will swell up inside the dog and cause great discomfort.

Fish can be substituted for one of the meat meals for a change on occasions. Herrings are particularly tasty and of excellent nutricious value and do not require to be filleted if cooked in a pressure cooker. If fed fairly regularly they certainly help to put a good bloom on the dog's coat. Never ever feed small bones such as chicken or rabbit but a large marrow bone will give your Setter hours of pleasure and it is of excellent value to the dog.

*A fine profile study of Cornevon Tokay bred by Mrs. L. M. Roberts (Photo: Diane Pearce)*

The Setter is not generally a greedy eater even from a puppy and when you first take him to his new home he may take a little time to settle to eat his meals properly. Do not let him dilly dally over his food. When he has had it for a reasonable time take it away from him if he has not finished it. Food should never be left lying around for your puppy to take when he wishes. Regular meal times must be adhered to at all times otherwise you will encourage him to be a faddy eater and make a rod for your own back. Regular feeding times are an essential kennel routine and all the meals should be given in a clean dish and not one that flies have been allowed to sample the leavings. A good supply of fresh water must always be available and kept in the same place so that the dog knows where to find it.

We have now looked into the matter of housing and feeding

your Setter so let us go to the equally important question of exercise.

**Exercise** Exercise is very important to your dog's health and happiness but do remember that as a puppy he should never leave your own domain until he has been fully inoculated. Until he is about four months of age all the exercise that he really requires he can get in his own home and garden. He must never be overexercised and as soon as he shows signs of tiring he should be allowed to go to his own bed and rest. He needs frequent rest periods to restore the mental energy as well as the physical energy that he uses up with his games and his frolics.

I stress strongly that children should not be encouraged to think of their dog as a plaything. He needs rest just as they do

*Sh. Ch. Laurie of Allsquare bred by Mr. James Johnson. (Photo Diane Pearce)*

and a mutual acceptanca of this is a good basis to work on. Puppies must be allowed to rest after their meal as quite obviously the weight of the food places a certain strain on their legs and if you wish them to mature properly then the puppy must be given this consideration.

As your dog grows up he will require more exercise of the proper type and an Irish Setter is an energetic dog and does want good free exercise in an open space. If this has to be your garden please ensure that it is securely fenced in so that he cannot escape. If it has to be in a communal park or common until he is fully trained put your Setter on a long lead or rope and let him gallop freely around until he has let off steam. He is a very active dog and should have a lot of scope in his movement and he simply must have this galloping exercise to allow him to develop properly and keep him both physically and mentally happy.

When an owner has more than one dog there is the decided advantage of the dogs playing together and help exercise themselves whether this be in a large run or in their own garden. The lone dog usually just sits at the gate of the run or at the back door of the house and waits to be taken into the house again.

Apart from this free range exercise road work is not only an important part of the Setter's exercise but it is an important part of his general training. It is during these sessions with his handler that he learns to respect and obey him and at the same time he is seeing and learning about things outside his own home and garden.

An under exercised adult house dog can quickly become a nuisance to his household. With not enough exercise to keep him happy he will think of other things to do. These things, unfortunately, are not always just appreciated in the home. Who wants chewed carpets, slippers or the children's toys? Coffee tables can easily be overturned when, in his exuberance, he rushes into the sitting room and equally doors can be badly scratched in his effort to be free to run. If your adult or near adult dog acquires such habits do not wonder why he is doing it. Look at your own exercising programme and ask yourself honestly if you are not slipping up on this important part of your dog's life. Exercise must be given whatever the weather, the state of your own health, the availability of time or even the Television programme. The odd day off here and there is, of course, acceptable but the fewer days off the better.

**Training** A young puppy only thinks of three things as being of any importance to him. Food, sleep and play. This is his world and it is the combination of these three things that must be used to train your dog.

The first essential for a house dog is for him to be taught to be clean in the house. This may present one or two minor problems and batties and it is here that discipline is very important. After each feed the puppy must be put outside to relieve himself. When he has done this he must be praised and at all times use his own name so that he knows it belongs to him. Bring him back straight into the house and by your tone of voice you can soon let him know that he has been a good dog. The rather long night can be a little bit of a problem but he will soon overcome this with your help.

Presuming that he has his bed in the kitchen put newspaper around it and encourage him to use this. When he attempts to relieve himself on another part of the floor lift him gently on to the newspaper and when he completes his little job then again give him praise. Gradually move the newspaper towards the door and the day will soon come when you can dispense with it and throw it outside. Of course a puppy is easier to house train in the summer than in the winter when so often the thought of going outside to both human and animal is not at all inviting.

There will be the odd mistakes and he will know that you are unhappy about thern and try not to do it again. De not scold severely for the first time or two and never scold him unless you catch him in the act as he just will not know what you are talking about. Do not confuse him with a lot of talk and only one person must talk to him at one time. It is no good the whole family screaming at him as this will only upset him and confuse him even further. Teach him the meaning of the simple words 'no' and 'yes' and as already advised use his own name to call him and praise him.

If you have to smack your puppy do not do it with your hand. He knows your hand as the one that feeds and pets him and you can destroy his trust in you. A rolled up newspaper is a very good substitute and a tap on the bottom with this and a few angry words will very soon indicate to him that all is not just right. Be fair with him at all times and do not scold one time for an offence and then ignore it the next time. This only bewilders a youngster and inconsistent training on your part will bring its own sorrows.

A puppy should be given his own toys such as an old slipper, a marrow bone from the butcher (never any other sort of bone) or one of the new safe rubber toys that are now on the market. If he has his own toys there is no earthly reason for him to borrow the children's toys or mother's best handbag and he must be scolded immediately found doing so. Take these things away from him and substitute them with his own possessions that he can chew to his heart's content. It will not take him long to learn what belongs to him and what does not.

Once he knows the aforegoing few simple rules and has comfortably established himself as part of the household then he must learn a little bit about collars and leads. This must never be left too late as the longer the lesson for both handler and dog is pushed into the background the greater the struggle it becomes.

While you are with him in the house and while he hardly notices it put a collar round his neck and watch for any reaction. So often nothing happens at all but sometimes he can take a great deal of exception to it and try to get it off. A larger dog, in my opinion, is easier to train to the lead than the

*Greenglades Golden Dream bred by Miss V. A. Albertis. (Photo Diane Pearce)*

toy dogs that really toss and turn in a desperate effort to reject the lead.

Never ever leave a collar on a dog and particularly a choke collar. There have a bad habit of getting caught up on posts or trees or things about the house and when a dog realises that he cannot escape he gets rather panicky and starts to struggle, twist and turn, in the hope of releasing himself. Very unfortunately this usually has the opposite effect and the offending object, the collar, tightens so much that the dog chokes himself. It is no good being warned after the tragedy it is best never to give it the opportunity to arise. A choke collar must be kept for his road exercise or his ring training. For normal use it is much better to use a good round leather type collar which is more comfortable for the dog.

When your puppy has become accustomed to the collar attach a lead to it and walk him up and down very carefully talking to him and encouraging him to come with you. He may sit on his bottom and be quite stubborn to begin with and you need all the patience in the world at this stage. This is not a game but a very important part of his training. Some puppies consider it fun and act rather like a bucking bronco and you may be rather amused by his antics. Nor for long, so do not let him get away with it—scold him firmly and he will realise it is not as funny as he thought it was. He will soon become accustomed to the lead and be quite prepared to co-operate with you and come to the demands that the lead makes upon him. From then on he can be trained to walk to heel, to stay and to the very useful command of 'down'. His progress can give you great satisfaction and if your dog has confidence in you he will respond quite quickly. It is absolutely essential that show dogs be trained these simple rules at an early age and his future career in the ring can depend upon this early training. Never be impatient with your Setter. He is a strong headed dog but is perfectly trainable and can be just as obedient as any obedience trained dog. Never lose his confidence through being unduly and perhaps not justifiably cross with him. If you once make him want to run away and hide from you do appreciate that you are on the way to losing the battle and it takes a great deal to win back his confidence.

If you wish to let him off in the country he must be fully trained never ever to think of chasing sheep, cattle or poultry or any other form of livestock. If he does chase after them do not blame the farmer using his shot gun, blame yourself for not keeping him properly under control.

If you feel that you are not getting on very well with the training of your setter and would like some helpful advice do not worry there are a lot of other people in the same boat with their dogs. There are many good training classes where both owner and dog can be educated. These classes are organised by one of the training organisations and are usually held about once a week. The whereabouts of these Clubs can be readily had from the Kennel Club.

*Sh. Ch. Minet Melody bred by Mr. G. G. Follows. (Photo: Diane Pearce)*

Apart from being good training centres you will meet all sorts of people and their dogs having the same problems as yourself. This in itself helps you feel better and these classes give not only you but your Setter an opportunity to meet other dogs of all sorts of breeds and further his education and yours too.

Do not think that if your progress with your dog's training is slow that it is the dog's fault. It could be but it is well to stop and think what perhaps you are doing wrong.

# Grooming and General Care of the Irish Setter

To get a good coat and keep a good coat on an Irish Setter it is essential that a correct diet is kept to. Unless the dog is fed properly once cannot expect to see a good result come out in the coat.

It is not essential to groom your Setter every day but his coat must be kept clear of dirt and muck that he may pick up whilst out exercising particularly on a wet day.

Grooming should start when the puppy is about three to four months old so that he can grow up accustomed to being handled and brushed. Brushing removes any dead hair and helps keep the new hair clean and healthy and in good condition. A Hound Glove is used by many people to groom their Setters and it proves most satisfactory. This glove has short bristles on one side and on the other side it has a material similar to corduroy or silk and after the initial grooming with the bristles the material on the other side of the glove finishes off by giving a lovely bloom to the coat. These gloves can be bought from any good pet shop or at dog shows.

Do not over wash your Setter as this, even when using the best shampoos on the market, tends to dry up the natural oils in the coat. If your Setter turns out to be a show dog never wash him immediately before a show. Do this two or three days before the show so that his coat will settle down to look neat and tidy for the day of the show. In the meantime, of course, you have to try and keep him out of the mud or the puddles which he seems to revel in just like any naughty child.

His fringes, i.e. under his tail, his chest and behind his legs require to be combed out. For this use a comb that does not have its teeth too close together and it should be about one inch in depth. Have patience when combing out these fringes and also the feather on the tail and try not to break the coat during this operation. When you have done all this your Irish Setter should look a very handsome dog and one that you should be very proud to own.

Never ever use scissors on a Setter's coat. The only exception to this rule is that if the hair grows rather excessively under the pads of the feet this can be neatly cut down between the toes and the pads. Never be too drastic with this operation as the Setter requires a certain amount of hair between the toes as a protection to his foot when he is exercised on rough ground and this particularly applies to dogs that are trained to work to the gun.

Show Setters are usually trimmed rather delicately around the ears to allow the ear to hang closer to the head. This should never be done with scissors and for the best effect the hair should be plucked out by finger and thumb. Many use stripping combs or thinning scissors for this operation but these can never better the old fashioned method of finger and thumb. This takes a bit longer to perform but I assure you it is well worth the extra trouble in the end.

Nails must be inspected occasionally but if your Setter is having regular road exercise or his run is part hard surface it is doubtful if his nails will require any attention at all. There are one or two different types of nail scissors or clippers available but I personally prefer the guillotine type because they are very simple and safe to use. If you do use them please be careful not to cut the quick as this can be very painful to the dog and will make him rather unwilling to have his feet handled by a judge if he is a show dog.

Teeth should be examined regularly. Sometimes the first eye teeth are rather reluctant to leave and it is wise to get your Veterinary Surgeon to remove them so that the second teeth can take over properly rather than try to grow in alongside the first teeth. If your Setter is a show prospect it is very impor-

47

tant that his second teeth should be allowed to grow in properly.

As your Setter grows older it may be that he will collect tartar round his teeth. If he is permitted to eat rough biscuits and chew marrow bones this is unlikely to happen but if he does take him along to your Veterinary Surgeon so that his teeth may be scaled.

Ears should be examined for cleanliness as so often and quite unnoticed little mites collect in them. This causes the ear to become inflamed and the dog begins to scratch it with resultant discomfort. Never push and prod into an ear. Handle them very carefully and if worried about excessive dirt or smell go to your Veterinary Surgeon straight away for the correct treatment.

Ear mites, fleas and such like are quite uninvited even in the best regulated canine families and it is no disgrace that your animal has collected them. If your dog is exercised in paddocks, fields or moors where the wild creatures of nature have been roaming it is quite likely that they will have left around these nasty mites and fleas that will be only too happy to settle on your dog. The main thing is to spot their presence right at the outset and take the correct steps to erradicate them immediately. It is surprising how quickly these strangers can settle in and take hold, and once established how difficult it is to get rid of them completely.

# Breeding and Whelping

Breeding is without doubt the most exciting part of keeping dogs. It is a great challenge that goes with breeding any sort of livestock from elephants to white mice. The pedigrees must be studied, the animals themselves, and it is the combination of the two that can produce your top winner. It is absolutely essential to know exactly what is behind your bitch's pedigree and the dog's pedigree and here, as a beginner, one must seek advice. The obvious place to turn to is the breeder of your bitch who should be well acquainted with at least what is behind your bitch.

It is no good setting off on your own course if you have no knowledge. The dog down the road is just not the right answer. When you consider the heartaches and disappointments that so often go with breeding a little thought about the planning of the litter is very much worthwhile.

Do seek advice on the best possible stud dog for your bitch. There are many things to consider. Your bitch must be a true respresentative of her breed with no major faults that she might pass on. It should always be your intention to improve on your bitch—this is what breeding is all about.

An Irish Setter takes a long time to come to full maturity and on no account should she be bred from on her first season. Normally Setters produce litters of about eight to ten, sometimes going up to fifteen. It is essential, therefore, to ensure that you have enough space either in the house or in an outside kennel to comfortably accommodate dam and family. If not then please do not attempt to have a litter from the bitch until your circumstances are such that adequate space is available. A nursing bitch must be able to have peace and quite and no expense can be spared with regard to her food and that of her puppies.

Do not get the mistaken idea that you will make a fortune from your litter. With ordinary luck you might just break even not taking into account your own time and labour. It is difficult to quote a hard and fast figure for the overall cost as there are so many factors that must be taken into consideration and with today's rising prices it is difficult to estimate. A summer litter is obviously cheaper to rear than a winter litter when heat is required. In trying to assess the approximate cost take into consideration the following factors—cost of stud fee and any travelling expenses incurred, cost of advertising the litter, cost of veterinary expenses, cost of heating, cost of food and, of course, your own time. In all I would say something in the region of just over £ 100 might cover it but with a big litter and perhaps having to hand rear at an earlier age it could be considerably more.

There are three methods of breeding. First there is In-Breeding, then Line-Breeding and thirdly. Out-Breeding. In this brief book on the Irish Setter there is not space to go into these methods in detail. If your appetite has been whetted there are many good books on the market that describe the intricacies of this complex subject in detail. There is no doubt, however, that it is a subject that even the beginner, if he or she wishes to succeed, should try to learn something about.

Briefly In-Breeding is the breeding of two animals very closely related such as Father to Daughter, Mother to Son, Brother to Sister etc. My advice on this is that it should be left to the experienced breeders who know exactly the make-up of the various pedigrees. It is quicker than line breeding but also much more dangerous to those without sufficient knowledge to apply it.

Line-Breeding is the mating of two dogs that have common ancestors and here again it is necessary to know these ancestors and to know their virtues and their faults.

Out-Breeding as it suggests is that the names on the pedigree bear no relationship to each other. It would be quite wrong to suggest that such matings have never been successful as we have had some top winners in the show ring that have come from this rather hit and miss combination. Such animals do not often, however, pass on to their progeny the same regular type that one expects from the more involved line-breeding and in-breeding.

It is well to remember that it is not always the Champions that produce the winners. In practically every breed one will find a dominant dog that for some reason or other has never commanded the title of Champion and yet has been a most successful sire producing champion children. One must never overlook such dogs and their pedigrees are well worthwhile studying.

In place of paying a stud fee it may be more convenient to you to request the owner of the stud dog to take a pick of the litter from your bitch. In my opinion this is not a very satisfactory method as so many things can go wrong such as the breeder taking the lovely puppy that you have set your heart on keeping. Pay your stud fee at the time of mating and then all the puppies are yours to do with what you want. Of course if the owner of the stud dog likes the look of a puppy you can always sell it if you do not want it yourself and the cost should be more than the charge of the stud fee.

Bitches vary as to when they should be mated. A careful watch must be kept on the bitch who will clearly indicate when the right time has come. This is usually from about the twelfth day onwards and when the discharge begins to lessen and becomes paler in colour. It is usual for the bitch to go to the dog and the owner of the dog will give advice on the best day to mate.

If you get a satisfactory mating there should be no call for a second one but if your bitch happens to miss most breeders will give a free service. Do not think that this is obligatory. This is merely a kindness on the part of the stud dog owner and if you get this matter quite clear when the mating takes place then there can be no misunderstanding. After your bitch has been safely mated please keep a carefull eye on her for another week. She will still attract followers and if she has not taken to the dog of your choice could easily have a mating of her own choice and produce a cross bred litter. If this does happen do not be worried by the old wife's tale that she will never again produce a pedigree litter. This is just a lot of nonsense and if mated again will produce a perfectly good Irish Setter litter.

Having got your bitch mated you now settle down to the long wait of nine weeks before the puppies arrive. Very little change will take place in the bitch for some weeks but very gradually the body will thicken and the milk glands nearest her hindquarters will become slightly swollen. During these first few weeks she must be treated just a she has been in the past with the same amount of exercise and food. Thereafter she should have an increase in her protein, i.e. her meat, and her carbohydrates, i.e. starch, should be cut down. Do not allow her to lead a sloppy life and get too fat and soft. This will hinder her when she actually whelps as she must be kept in good hard muscular condition to ensure a natural and easy whelping.

As the bitch gets nearer to her time of whelping, i.e. about the seventh week, allow her to go for her walks at her own pace and stop her going up and down stairs or jumping on to boxes or settees. This bumping up and down is hardly likely to do the whelps any good. When it is obvious that she is carrying a good sized litter split her meals up and instead of one make them into two smaller ones, or even three, giving her additional protein foods. During the latter weeks the movement of the whelps will be noticeable and care must be taken not to get the expectant mum over tired.

Introduce her to the whelping quarters about ten days before she is due to whelp. Sixty-three days is the actual period of gestation but bitches can whelp anything up to five or six days early and three or four days late. Keep a constant watch on her and if you are all worried about her condition do contact your Veterinary Surgeon at once. Any nasty discharge should be attended to immediately or the consequences could be very serious. Let your Veterinary Surgeon know that you have a bitch about to whelp so that if you have to call him in the middle of the night—bitches have a habit of choosing this sort of time to whelp—then at least he has been warned.

The bitch's bed should be a strong wooden one with a rail fitted around the inside of the box about two inches from the ground. (See diagram)

This will permit the puppies to crawl beneath it when they are very young and it does help to save a puppy that might have been squashed by an inexperienced mum. Do not blame her if she does have just such an accident. Remember she is a big girl in comparison to the small whelps and so often a maiden bitch will find the whole operation just a little difficult to cope with and the rail can be of great help to her at this time.

The best method of heating I have found to be a tubular electric heater placed in beneath the bed taking care that all electric wires are as safely quarded against the bitch getting at them as possible. If an infra red lamp is used it should not be

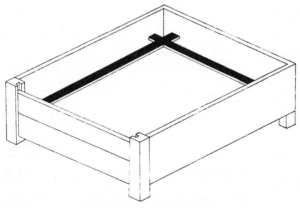

*Whelping Box with guard rail.*

*A large litter of ten puppies seen with their dam Coolavins Nanno.*

too low as they can cause the mother discomfort and are not particularly good for her coat. Unless the weather is terribly cold we prefer the under bed method and it seems to me that the whelps do to.

Newspaper is by far the best thing for your bitch to whelp on and as your bitch gets to her due date she will scrape the paper up and really get quite frantic in her efforts to make her bed. This is quite normal if it happens near her date so do not be alarmed by this behaviour. A day before whelping she will probably refuse her food and if her temperature is taken it will have dropped down below normal. Her temperature can be taken by gently twisting a thermometer that has had its end greased in vaseline into her rectum. Normal temperature is about 38.6°C or 101.5°F.

The first signs of a puppy about to arrive are when the bitch starts to strain and as the straining gets more pronounced and with shorter periods in between you should expect the puppy to make its appearance. Inexperienced bitches can become a little worried at this stage and it is nice for them to have their owner with them just to gently reassure them that all is well. I never leave my bitches to whelp on their own as there are so many things that could go wrong but that can be put right if someone is with them. With a maiden bitch it could be that you will have to help her sever the cord that is attached to the puppy and the afterbirth. Have ready a blunt pair of sterilised scissors and you can quite quickly nip off the cord about a couple of inches from the puppy's tummy. The bitch will be so busy licking and attending to her new charges that she will hardly notice your intravention. If she wants to grab the afterbirth and eat it let her have her own way as this is a natural reaction and what she would do in wild life. The bitch's own natural instincts are quite quiet and calm and interfere as little as possible mother nature will carry your bitch through this normal function with ease and a calm efficiency. In between each puppy it may be that she would like some heated milk with a little glucose added. This will help her on her way. Never offer her any solid food at this time.

If you feel that perhaps she is having some difficulty in passing a whelp do not interfere yourself until you have gained a great deal of experience. Call your Veterinary Surgeon. Once she has started she should continue to have her puppies at fairly regular intervals. She may, however, have one or two quite closely together and then have a fair gap of an hour or even two before she produces another puppy. This is quite normal. Keep a fairly rough clean towel handy as if a puppy seems to be a little slow in coming to and showing activity lift it up in the towel and give it quite a vigorous rub and massage. They are really quite tough so do not be afraid to give it this treatment. When you hear it scream then it is well on its way to life and should be allowed to join the gang and let mother continue the good work.

## GESTATION TABLE

*Showing when your bitch is due to whelp*

| MATED JANUARY | DUE TO WHELP MARCH | MATED FEBRUARY | DUE TO WHELP APRIL | MATED MARCH | DUE TO WHELP MAY | MATED APRIL | DUE TO WHELP JUNE | MATED MAY | DUE TO WHELP JULY | MATED JUNE | DUE TO WHELP AUGUST | MATED JULY | DUE TO WHELP SEPTEMBER | MATED AUGUST | DUE TO WHELP OCTOBER | MATED SEPTEMBER | DUE TO WHELP NOVEMBER | MATED OCTOBER | DUE TO WHELP DECEMBER | MATED NOVEMBER | DUE TO WHELP JANUARY | MATED DECEMBER | DUE TO WHELP FEBRUARY |
|---|---|---|---|---|---|---|---|---|---|---|---|---|---|---|---|---|---|---|---|---|---|---|---|
| 1 | 5 | 1 | 5 | 1 | 3 | 1 | 3 | 1 | 3 | 1 | 3 | 1 | 2 | 1 | 3 | 1 | 3 | 1 | 3 | 1 | 3 | 1 | 2 |
| 2 | 6 | 2 | 6 | 2 | 4 | 2 | 4 | 2 | 4 | 2 | 4 | 2 | 3 | 2 | 4 | 2 | 4 | 2 | 4 | 2 | 4 | 2 | 3 |
| 3 | 7 | 3 | 7 | 3 | 5 | 3 | 5 | 3 | 5 | 3 | 5 | 3 | 4 | 3 | 5 | 3 | 5 | 3 | 5 | 3 | 5 | 3 | 4 |
| 4 | 8 | 4 | 8 | 4 | 6 | 4 | 6 | 4 | 6 | 4 | 6 | 4 | 5 | 4 | 6 | 4 | 6 | 4 | 6 | 4 | 6 | 4 | 5 |
| 5 | 9 | 5 | 9 | 5 | 7 | 5 | 7 | 5 | 7 | 5 | 7 | 5 | 6 | 5 | 7 | 5 | 7 | 5 | 7 | 5 | 7 | 5 | 6 |
| 6 | 10 | 6 | 10 | 6 | 8 | 6 | 8 | 6 | 8 | 6 | 8 | 6 | 7 | 6 | 8 | 6 | 8 | 6 | 8 | 6 | 8 | 6 | 7 |
| 7 | 11 | 7 | 11 | 7 | 9 | 7 | 9 | 7 | 9 | 7 | 9 | 7 | 8 | 7 | 9 | 7 | 9 | 7 | 9 | 7 | 9 | 7 | 8 |
| 8 | 12 | 8 | 12 | 8 | 10 | 8 | 10 | 8 | 10 | 8 | 10 | 8 | 9 | 8 | 10 | 8 | 10 | 8 | 10 | 8 | 10 | 8 | 9 |
| 9 | 13 | 9 | 13 | 9 | 11 | 9 | 11 | 9 | 11 | 9 | 11 | 9 | 10 | 9 | 11 | 9 | 11 | 9 | 11 | 9 | 11 | 9 | 10 |
| 10 | 14 | 10 | 14 | 10 | 12 | 10 | 12 | 10 | 12 | 10 | 12 | 10 | 11 | 10 | 12 | 10 | 12 | 10 | 12 | 10 | 12 | 10 | 11 |
| 11 | 15 | 11 | 15 | 11 | 13 | 11 | 13 | 11 | 13 | 11 | 13 | 11 | 12 | 11 | 13 | 11 | 13 | 11 | 13 | 11 | 13 | 11 | 12 |
| 12 | 16 | 12 | 16 | 12 | 14 | 12 | 14 | 12 | 14 | 12 | 14 | 12 | 13 | 12 | 14 | 12 | 14 | 12 | 14 | 12 | 14 | 12 | 13 |
| 13 | 17 | 13 | 17 | 13 | 15 | 13 | 15 | 13 | 15 | 13 | 15 | 13 | 14 | 13 | 15 | 13 | 15 | 13 | 15 | 13 | 15 | 13 | 14 |
| 14 | 18 | 14 | 18 | 14 | 16 | 14 | 16 | 14 | 16 | 14 | 16 | 14 | 15 | 14 | 16 | 14 | 16 | 14 | 16 | 14 | 16 | 14 | 15 |
| 15 | 19 | 15 | 19 | 15 | 17 | 15 | 17 | 15 | 17 | 15 | 17 | 15 | 16 | 15 | 17 | 15 | 17 | 15 | 17 | 15 | 17 | 15 | 16 |
| 16 | 20 | 16 | 20 | 16 | 18 | 16 | 18 | 16 | 18 | 16 | 18 | 16 | 17 | 16 | 18 | 16 | 18 | 16 | 18 | 16 | 18 | 16 | 17 |
| 17 | 21 | 17 | 21 | 17 | 19 | 17 | 19 | 17 | 19 | 17 | 19 | 17 | 18 | 17 | 19 | 17 | 19 | 17 | 19 | 17 | 19 | 17 | 18 |
| 18 | 22 | 18 | 22 | 18 | 20 | 18 | 20 | 18 | 20 | 18 | 20 | 18 | 19 | 18 | 20 | 18 | 20 | 18 | 20 | 18 | 20 | 18 | 19 |
| 19 | 23 | 19 | 23 | 19 | 21 | 19 | 21 | 19 | 21 | 19 | 21 | 19 | 20 | 19 | 21 | 19 | 21 | 19 | 21 | 19 | 21 | 19 | 20 |
| 20 | 24 | 20 | 24 | 20 | 22 | 20 | 22 | 20 | 22 | 20 | 22 | 20 | 21 | 20 | 22 | 20 | 22 | 20 | 22 | 20 | 22 | 20 | 21 |
| 21 | 25 | 21 | 25 | 21 | 23 | 21 | 23 | 21 | 23 | 21 | 23 | 21 | 22 | 21 | 23 | 21 | 23 | 21 | 23 | 21 | 23 | 21 | 22 |
| 22 | 26 | 22 | 26 | 22 | 24 | 22 | 24 | 22 | 24 | 22 | 24 | 22 | 23 | 22 | 24 | 22 | 24 | 22 | 24 | 22 | 24 | 22 | 23 |
| 23 | 27 | 23 | 27 | 23 | 25 | 23 | 25 | 23 | 25 | 23 | 25 | 23 | 24 | 23 | 25 | 23 | 25 | 23 | 25 | 23 | 25 | 23 | 24 |
| 24 | 28 | 24 | 28 | 24 | 26 | 24 | 26 | 24 | 26 | 24 | 26 | 24 | 25 | 24 | 26 | 24 | 26 | 24 | 26 | 24 | 26 | 24 | 25 |
| 25 | 29 | 25 | 29 | 25 | 27 | 25 | 27 | 25 | 27 | 25 | 27 | 25 | 26 | 25 | 27 | 25 | 27 | 25 | 27 | 25 | 27 | 25 | 26 |
| 26 | 30 | 26 | 30 | 26 | 28 | 26 | 28 | 26 | 28 | 26 | 28 | 26 | 27 | 26 | 28 | 26 | 28 | 26 | 28 | 26 | 28 | 26 | 27 |
| 27 | 31 | 27 | May 1 | 27 | 29 | 27 | 29 | 27 | 29 | 27 | 29 | 27 | 28 | 27 | 29 | 27 | 29 | 27 | 29 | 27 | 29 | 27 | 28 |
| 28 | Apl 1 | 28 | 2 | 28 | 30 | 28 | 30 | 28 | 30 | 28 | 30 | 28 | 29 | 28 | 30 | 28 | 30 | 28 | 30 | 28 | 30 | 28 | Mar 1 |
| 29 | 2 | 29 | 3 | 29 | 31 | 29 | July 1 | 29 | 31 | 29 | 31 | 29 | 30 | 29 | 31 | 29 | Dec 1 | 29 | 31 | 29 | 31 | 29 | 2 |
| 30 | 3 | — | — | 30 | June 1 | 30 | 2 | 30 | Aug 1 | 30 | Sept 1 | 30 | Oct 1 | 30 | Nov 1 | 30 | 2 | 30 | Jan 1 | 30 | Feb 1 | 30 | 3 |
| 31 | 4 | — | — | 31 | 2 | — | — | 31 | 2 | — | — | 31 | 2 | 31 | 2 | — | — | 31 | 2 | — | — | 31 | 4 |

It sometimes does happen that the bitch does not feel in the slightest maternal and it is here that the experienced breeder must act quickly. For those less experienced the only solution is your Veterinary Surgeon who will instruct you on the correct procedure for the arrival of the whelps. After attending the arrival of one or two whelps it may be that you can continue on your own.

It is not always easy to determine when the last puppy has arrived particularly in a big roomy bitch but no harm is done if the bitch is removed from her whelping bed and taken out into the garden for a quick walk and given the opportunity to relieve herself.

Bitches are reluctant to leave the scene of all their labours and understandably so but put a collar and lead on and persuade her to go out even for a very brief moment.

When she is absent get another pair of hands to quickly collect all the soiled paper and replace it with new. In doing this it is quickest to put the whelps into an already prepared box transferring them as soon as the new paper is laid.

Normalily when a bitch is finished whelping she will stretch out with her whelps letting them all into her teats and there is no lovelier sight than a full house of new arrivals with a contented mum. If she tends to be restless and keeps moving her position and seems uncomfortable it may be that an after-birth or even another puppy has not come away. This can cause serious trouble but can quickly be rectified by an injection of pituitarin given by your Veterinary Surgeon.

The bitch should be kept on a light diet for the first two days, i.e. plenty of milk foods with glucose added. After this, if everything seems normal, she should gradually go back to a full quota of meat and meal with cod liver oil and bone meal added.

At about three to four days dew claws should be removed by your Veterinary Surgeon. This is optional but as dew claws have a nasty habit of catching on to all sorts of things they are far better removed as they serve no useful purpose and in an older dog if they get caught up in the undergrowth or hedgerows whilst out exercising can get badly torn necessitating stitching.

Keep a close eye on the puppies' nails as with a big litter they can cause unnecessary discomfort to the bitch as they grow older. See that they are kept short and cared for otherwise the bitch's tummy will be covered in scars and scratches. Nails should be trimmed about once a week from about ten days. It is easy at this stage to avoid the quick which is pink and only the rounded white tip should be clipped. When the puppy gets on his own legs and starts getting about on hard surfaces this job will not be necessary and his nails should require little further attention.

At about three weeks your puppies should be weaned as if you have a big litter they will have drained their dam quite considerably. Do make sure that the bitch is having enough to eat plus a good supply of fresh milk if she will drink it. Fresh water must always be available. The quantity of food given to your bitch must depend on the number of puppies she is rearing. When you start to feed the puppies you must not think that you can cut down on your bitch's food. She has a very long way to go in the rearing of her litter and will be under strain for many weeks to come.

Start the whelps by giving them a small quantity of scraped raw meat. Put this in your hand and you will be surprised how quickly they catch on to this idea. Their noses will lead them to it and it is seldom that they need much teaching. Gradually increase the amount of meat each day by the beginning of the fourth week they are having two meals of meat with cod liver oil and bone meal added. It is best to feed them separately at this stage as in every litter there are the greedy puppies and the bullies and the not so greedy and more retiring members. I find that milk foods are best introduced after the second meat meal has been established.

Puppies are inclined to get themselves in a terrible mess with the sloppy milk meals and so often lose more than they take

*Monty Court of Medena bred by Mr. D. Harris. (Photo: Diane Pearce)*

which is a waste. With the continual gradual increase of the puppies food they will not quite make the same demands on the bitch and the whole process of changing over from dam to ordinary food should be done so easily and gently that it should hardly be noticeable to either the bitch or the puppies.

During the weaning period it is a good thing to have, in the whelping quarters, an upturned box or platorm that the bitch is able to jump on to and yet too high for the puppies to make demands on her. In this way she can get away from her babies when and is she wants to. One can imagine that with a big litter she is glad to escape from the little rascals on occasions and yet able to keep her eye on them.

The puppies should be treated for worms at about three weeks of age and then again about five or six weeks of age. Tablets for this can be prescribed by your Veterinary Surgeon and do be careful to get precise instructions for their use. Nowadays they have little effect on the puppies except to help eradicate the worms so that no ill effects should become present.

As the puppies grow on they should be fed communally in two or three dishes. Do make sure that they all get a fair share. Lift the greedy ones away and give the more genteel eaters longer time to finish their meal. Unless you do this you will finish up with an uneven litter which is just not the best advertisement for good rearing.

There is a great deal of pleasure in rearing any litter but the first litter when everything is new to you must always be remembered as something special. Every member of that litter is a character in his or her own right and by the time the puppies are ready to go to their new homes you will remember them all for some little individuality. It is rather a sad day, particularly for a new breeder, when the day comes to part with the puppies that you have known so well and that you should be so proud to have bred and reared.

Make sure that their next great big step into the outside world is made as simple as possible for them and their new owners. Make sure, as far as you can, that they are going to the sort of home that you would wish for them. Make sure that you have sent each puppy off with all his papers and more important still that a diet sheet goes with the puppy and that you have taken time to carefully explain it to the new owners. You have now bred and sold your first litter. How do you feel about it? Are you now planning your next one? I hope so.

# Showing the Irish Setter

This yet another most exciting part of keeping dogs and depending just how seriously one takes it can be very time absorbing and, of course, expensive.

Details of shows in the U.K. can be found in the Dog Papers, *Our Dogs* and *Dog World* and, of course, from the Kennel Club who publish a monthly magazine called the *Kennel Club Gazette* which lists all the shows months ahead.

In Britain there are three different types of shows and as a beginner I would advise you to start off with the Limited or Members' Shows graduating to the Open and Championship Shows if you find that your dog is good enough. Competition in this country is very keen and it is just a waste of money if your dog does not come up to this expectation. On the other hand if you have a good dog, well presented, even the most humble novice can get to the top and it is a very exciting road.

**Limited Shows** These are shows at which the entry is limited to members of clubs or societies or to exhibitors from within a specified area. These shows are much smaller than Open Shows but are very well supported particularly with young stock and can draw well over 100 entries. They are excellent grounds for training puppies and owners. Champions or dogs that have won a Challenge Certificate towards their Championship are not permitted to enter.

**Open Shows** These shows have no restrictions and certainly at the bigger Open Shows many champions do appear. In Britain these shows can be very big with over fifty different breeds scheduled and bigger than many Championship Shows in other countries. It is at these shows that judges gain the further experience necessary for them to qualify as Championship Show Judges.

**Championship Shows** These are benched Open Shows at which the Kennel Club Challenge Certificates are offered. These are the most important of all and their awards are eagerly sought. Three of these Challenge Certificates under three different judges is the qualification for a Champion. At no other show than a Championship Show can you qualify your dog for this award. It is generally regarded that it is harder to make up a Champion in Britain than in any other country.

Write to the Secretary of the show that you wish to attend for a schedule. Read this carefully and abide by all its rules and regulations and do see that you get your entry form completed and returned to the Secretary in good time.

If the show chosen is benched you will require a blanket and a benching chain. Before attending a benched show it is a good idea to give your dog a little experience so that he does not create unwelcome noises because he finds himself tied up to something that he cannot get away from. Put a benching chain

*Breed Specialist Mrs. M. Stephens inspects Shadancy Mudlark. (Photo: Diane Pearce)*

*Goldings Joss Cambier wins his 2nd C.C. much to the delight of his proud owner. (Photo: Diane Pearce)*

on to his leather collar, never a choke chain, and attach him to a tree in the garden or a table leg in the house. He will soon get used to the idea and settle on his bench at the show. Be patient with him for the first few times and do not leave him unnecessarily until you are quite sure that he knows what it is all about. For obvious reasons, as explained in an earlier chapter, the choke chain could be disastrous. Exhibitors are very busy people at shows and if you happen to be absent from your bench when your Setter is in trouble do not assume that because there are plenty of people around that his trouble will be attended to. Of course it will be if it is noticed but do not rely on this happening.

Every exhibitor carries a show bag in which are kept the requirements for the show. These consist of a benching rug, benching chain, bowl for water, biscuits for your dog to chew on the bench, your grooming kit, towels to dry your Setter with if it is wet and perhaps some tit-bits that he has been

*Golden Joss Cambier, seen on previous page, in exhibition stance. (Photo: Diane Pearce)*

*Sh. Ch. Twoacres Traviata bred by Mrs. J. E. Coates. (Photo: Diane Pearce)*

*Two puppies relaxing in their spotless pen*

*This girl is enjoying the company of her affectionate friend.*

*Being of an inquisitive nature, these two peek out from their owners window.*

*A study of a fine specimen.*

*A welcome rest after a good romp.*

*Irish Setters are very loving towards their litters.*

*Sh. Ch. Corriecas Baron bred by Mrs. B. Levick. (Photo: Diane Pearce)*

*Pack Major of Allsquare bred by Mr. J. M. Johnson.*

taught to show for in the ring. It is also a good idea to carry a small towel and some soap for yourself to have a clean-up with as on muddy days this can be most necessary. If your dog prefers milk then a plastic bottle of milk should be taken with you. Your dog should be taken to the show with a good type round collar and a strong leather or nylon lead.

If the show is unbenched you will be permitted to leave your dog in the car until it is time to get him off to groom him for his class. If the day is hot he must not be left in the car and should be brought into the hall or if it is outside to settle down beside you to await his class.

Once your Setter has settled on his bench offer him something to drink. He may not want it but he should at least be given the opportunity. If your dog is a bad traveller you must allow yourself plenty of time to get to the show so that he has good time to settle before he has to go into the ring. There are many good remedies on the market today for dogs that do not travel without sickness. Few dogs are unhappy on their bench. Just watch how all the old hands eagerly jump on to their bench and settle down very quickly. When settled give your Setter a biscuit or two to chew—this helps keep him happy.

You should have done all your grooming at home so that all that is necessary is to put the finishing touches to your dog. You must work out just how long that will take so that you are quite ready and prepared to go into the ring when required.

You will have trained your dog at home and no doubt at the training classes so that you are prepared to meet the demands of the judge. You have practised the best way to make your dog show and whether or not to use a little bit of liver or some other delicacy to hold his attention. You are, therefore, quite ready to repeat this in the show ring. Try not to be nervous as your own tension has a habit of running down the lead and conveying this to your dog and then neither of you will give your best. Watch what the other exhibitors have been asked to do when moving their dogs and follow this procedure as

*Sh. Ch. Marrona Merriel bred by Mrs. M. E. Stokes is seen here with one of many cups won. The beautiful sheen on the coat indicates the care and attention given to this by the owner. (Photo: Diane Pearce)*

this is obviously the way the judge wants it done. Having moved your dog go back to where the steward directs, await further instructions. Most judges will bring five or six dogs into the ring for a final selection and if you are not chosen to stay leave the ring immediately. The judge's time today, with the large entries at shows, is very limited and any hindrance can cause annoyance and delay to a busy judge. If you are lucky you will receive your prize card and thereafter you will leave the ring when instructed by the steward. It may be, however, that you have not had any recognition and you leave the ring empty handed. Do not be disappointed as this is only one person's opinion — there is always another day- The judge is the important person on the day. Usually they are most considerate, especially to new comers, but try to obey their instructions and never speak to the judge unless he or she speaks to you.

It is a good idea to purchase a catalogue immediately on arrival at the show as this will give all details as to time and what ring you are required to show your dog in. Check it as soon as possible to make sure that your entry is scheduled. If not consult the Secretary straight away. When you enter the ring you will be given your ring number by the steward and this you attach to yourself with a pin or a special clip that is available from most stalls at the show. Stand in the ring where the steward directs you and await your turn for the judge's verdict. Let us hope that you have success with your showing and I must warn you that if you do it is a most infectious success and it will find you travelling many miles in search of it. There is a marvellous comradeship amongst exhibitors and you will make many new friends all with the same common interest—the dog.

As far as dog show competition etc. in the States is concerned I again like to quote Mrs. Luz. Holderstot. She says:

## TYPES OF DOG SHOWS

There are various types of dog shows. The American Kennel

Club sanctioned matches are shows at which purebred dogs may compete, but not for championship points. These are excellent for you to enter to accustom you and your dog to showing. If your dog places in a few match shows, then you might seriously consider entering the big-time shows. An American Kennel Club all-breed show is one at which purebred dogs compete for championship points. An American Kennel Club specialty show is for one breed only. It may be held in conjunction with an all-breed show (by designating the classes at that show as its specialty show) or it may be held entirely apart. Obedience trials are different in that in them the dog is judged according to his obedience and ability to perform, not by his conformation to the breed standard.

There are two types of championship conformation shows: *benched* and *unbenched*. At a benched show your dog must be on his appointed bench during the advertised hours of the show's duration. He may be removed from the bench only to be taken to the exercise pen or to be groomed (an hour before the showing) in an area designated for handlers to set up their crates and grooming tables. At an unbenched show your car may serve as a bench for your dog.

To become a champion your dog must win fifteen points in competition with other dogs; a portion of the fifteen points must be awarded as major point wins (three to five points) under different judges.

## HOW TO ENTER

If your dog is purebred and registered with the AKC—or eligible for registration—you may enter him in the appropriate show class for which his age, sex, and previous show record qualify him. You will find coming shows listed in the different dog magazines or at your petshop. Write to the secretary of the show, asking for the premium list. When you receive the entry form, fill it in carefully and send it back with the required entry fee. Then, before the show, you should receive your exhibitor's pass, which will admit you and your dog to the show. Here are the five official show classes:

PUPPY CLASS: Open to dogs at least six months and not more than twelve months of age. Limited to dogs whelped in the United States and Canada.

NOVICE CLASS: Open to dogs six months of age or older that have never won a first prize in any class other than puppy class, and less than three first prizes in the novice class itself. Limited to dogs whelped in the United States or Canada.

BRED BY EXHIBITOR CLASS: Open to all dogs, except champions, six months of age or over which are exhibited by the same person, or his immediate family, or kennel that was the recognized breeder on the records of the American Kennel Club.

AMERICAN-BRED CLASS: Open to dogs that are not champions, six months of age or over, whelped in the United states after a mating which took place in the United States.

OPEN CLASS: Open to dogs six months of age or over, with no exceptions.

In addition there are local classes, the Specials Only class, and brace and team entries.

## JUNIOR SHOWMANSHIP

If you have considered that you and your dog are going to go the show route, you might consider having your youngster show the dog in the ring. If your child has an especially good relationship with his pet, or if he has trained the dog himself, as many children do, then Junior Showmanship might be a good learning experience.

Junior Showmanship is competition among children of different age groups, handling dogs owned by their immediate families. The age divisions are: Novice A, for 10 to 12 year olds; Novice B, for those boys and girls from 13 to 16 (entrants in these two classes must have one or no prior Junior Showmanship wins); Open A for those 10 to 12 years of age;

Open B for those 13 to 16 (these entrants must have earned two or more Junior Showmanship awards).

Children involved in JS have the wonderful opportunity to feel a sense of achievement and victory, should they walk away with the ribbons after a show. Even still, winning is not the most important factor here; the pride and responsibility the youngster feels at having reached the ring is surely worth the effort and discipline required to enter showmanship competition.

For more information on JS, and to obtain a rules and regulations booklet, you can contact the American Kennel Club in New York.

## ADVANCED PREPARATION

Before you go to a show your dog should be trained to gait at a trot beside you, with head up and in a straight line. In the ring you will have to gait your dog around the edge with other dogs and then individually up and down the center runner. In addition the dog must stand for examination by the judge, who will look at him closely and feel his head and body structure. He should be taught to stand squarely, hind feet slightly back, head up on the alert. Showing requires practice training sessions in advance. Get a friend to act as judge and set the dog up and 'show' him a few minutes every day.

Sometime before the show, give your dog a bath so he will look his best. Get together all the things you will need no take to the show. You will want to take a water dish and a bottle of water for your dog (so he won't be affected by a change in drinking water). Take your show lead, bench chain (if it is a benched show), combs and brush, and the identification ticket sent by the show superintendent, noting the time you must be there and the place where the show will be held, as well as the time of judging.

# THE DAY OF THE SHOW

Don't feed your dog the morning of the show, or give him at most a light meal. He will be more comfortable in the car on the way, and will show more enthusiastically. When you arrive at the show grounds, find out where he is to be benched and settle him there. Your bench or stall number is on your identification ticket, and the breed name will be on placards fastened to the ends of the row of benches. Once you have your dog securely fastened to his stall by a bench chain (use a bench crate instead of a chain if you prefer), locate the ring where your dog will be judged (the number and time of showing will be on the program of judging which came with your ticket). After this you may want to take your dog to the exercise ring to relieve himself, and give him a small drink of water. Your dog will have been groomed before the show, but give him a final brushing just before going into the show ring. When your breed judging is called, it is your responsibility to be at the ringside ready to go in. The steward will give you an armband which has on it the number of your dog.

Then, as you step into the ring, try to keep your knees from knocking! Concentrate on your dog and before you realize it you'll be out again, perhaps back with the winners of each class for more judging and finally, with luck, it will be over and you'll have a ribbon and trophy—and, of course, the most wonderful dog in the world!

# The Irish Setter in Work

All gundogs have their specific job when it comes to their work in the field and with the gun. The Setter or Pointer has the job of finding the game which on discovery he 'points out' to the 'guns'. To do this he must be able to cover a great range of ground and pick up the airborne scent of the birds. The Irish Setter must be developed to travel fast with his head held high to pick up the scent of the birds before they realise that he is on their trail and have the opportunity to fly off to safety. On picking up the bird-scent the dog should come to a complete stop and almost freeze in position with his head pointing to where the bird is resting. The dog should stay quite stiff and rigid until either the bird is disturbed by some little noise or movement and flies away or one of the 'guns' approaches and this position of the dog is called the 'point'.

There is nothing nicer than to see an Irish Setter working properly and well and with a keen interest. He has a very beautiful style with his noble head held high and his wide nostrils straining to pick up the scent. He is incredibly free in his movement and the gay lashing of his tail really makes a very satisfying picture. It has been written many times, in the years gone by, that he is a very head strong dog and quite often difficult to control in work but most would readily agree that if he is kept in work and at it, that there is no better companion to the gun.

As the dog stiffens to 'point' it is not fallacy but true that for some extraordinary reason the game selected seems to become completely paralysed and almost hypnotised and incapable of moving. When this position is disturbed and the trance broken the bird flies off and the gun is fired. The Irish Setter's job should then be finished and he should drop to the ground and lie quite still until he receives instructions from his handler. It is at this point that the Retrievers take over and retrieve the wounded or dead game.

It is true to say, unfortunately, that only a small percentage of today's show Setter are trained to work and it seems to me that as this natural gift of finding game is so instinctive to these dogs it is a great pity that more of them are not given the opportunity to be trained to this work. To stifle this instinctive ability and to leave it lying dormant cannot help to develop the really true characteristics of the Irish Setter. Let us never forget that the sporting Irishmen of years gone by revelled in the Irish Setter's great ability in the field and bred them to develop this all important part of their character. Let us try not to destroy it.

Let us hope that perhaps some of the new owners and breeders of the Irish Setter will make an effort to train their dog. There are many excellent Gundog Training Clubs that will give all the help necessary to those willing to train their dog and be trained themselves. The names of these Clubs can be had from the Kennel Club or from one of the Breed Clubs listed at the end of this book. Do make use of the facilities and training they offer and I assure you that the pleasure you will get from training your Irish Setter to work in the field will not only be satisfying to you and your dog but most exhilarating.

For those more interested in Obedience Work I would advise joining an Obedience Training Club. Here again you will find it most interesting to work your dog and train him to a high degree of obedience. The names and addresses of the Clubs can, once again, be had from the Kennel Club.

Give your Irish Setter something real to think about, and to do, and it will certainly help keep him out of mischief.

# The Health of the Irish Setter

There are so many good books written nowadays on the subject of health in our canine friends that I feel this subject should be left to the Veterinary Surgeons.

The Irish Setter is normally a very healthy dog if looked after properly and should go through life without giving any real concern over his health.

There is the question of accidents and it might be well here just to have a look at one or two of the more common incidents that could happen to your Setter.

**Bites** If your dog is bitten by another animal cleanse the wound and apply penicillin ointment or tincture of Iodine. It is important that the wound should be kept open until all discharge stops. Thereafter a healing ointment can be applied.

**Burns and Scalds** Unless these are of a minor nature they should be treated by your Veterinary Surgeon as soon as possible. There is always the question of shock no matter how slight the accident. Clean the burn and remove any foreign material such as dirt, straw, hair, food etc. Exclude all air by applying a dressing soaked in a strong solution of tea. Many households now carry in their kitchen cupboard lotions to apply in the case of a first degree burn to a human, and the same lotions can be applied to dogs when the burn is a minor one.

**External Haemorrhage** In the case of an accident exessive bleeding can be controlled by bandaging dry cotton wool firmly over the injury. If this is not successful a tourniquet may be required until professional aid can be obtained. A handkerchief, stocking or something similar should be tied tightly around the part above the injury and then tightened by putting a stick or pencil through and twisting until the flow of blood lessens. Tourniquets must be removed every ten minutes.

**Poisoning** Great speed must be employed to expel any poison swallowed by a dog. Simple emetics are the best, e.g. washing soda or salt and water. If the dog has been stung by a bee the sting should be extracted if possible. The spot should then be treated with T.C.P. or carbonate of soda. If stung by a wasp the wound should be treated with vinegar or acid and in both cases it is advisable to have the animal injected with antihistamine for a quick result.

**Shock** This occurs after severe injury in an accident of one sort or another. The dog must be kept as quiet as possible and warm. A dog that is not fully conscious should never be persuaded to swallow any liquid. If it is able to swallow naturally and without choking then a drop of brandy of whisky in water is very helpful.

**Snakes Bites** Very few snake bites in this country are serious. Adders do spring up now and again and if your dog is bitten by an adder take action straight away. A bandage should be applied as tightly as possible above the part bitten and between the bite and the heart. This prevents the poison spreading into the bloodstream. Open up the bite and push into it crystals of permanganate of potash and call your Veterinary Surgeon. Keep your dog as comfortable as possible and here again a little brandy will not hurt.

**Sunstroke or Heatstroke** Always see that your dog has a good supply of water in his run and if he has to be left out in his run for any length of time he must have adequate shade. In a hot summer sunstroke is not at all unusual. The signs are excessive panting with profuse salivation followed by weakness of the limbs almost a staggering gait and then complete collapse. Put the dog into a cool place at once and apply ice and cold water to his head, neck and shoulders. I once saved a well known dog by simply plunging him into a tank of cold water with just his head above the surface. Keep him

*A fine head study of Wellington Meadowsweet bred by Mrs. K. and Miss J. Norman. (Photo: Diane Pearce)*

there for just a few minutes and then remove him to a quiet cool area and give him a drink. It is amazing how quickly the dog will come round if you catch him in time.

**Wounds** Never bandage a wound unless it is absolutely necessary as the dog will always try to take off the bandages and in doing so may further damage the wound. If a bandage is necessary then take the precaution of attaching a plastic bucket, with the bottom cut out, to the dog's collar. This will stop him from getting at the wound. It may be uncomfortable for the dog but it does allow the wound to heal much quicker. All serious wounds should always be attended to by your Veterinary Surgeon.

*Twoacres Teresa bred by Mrs. J. E. Coates. (Photo: Diane Pearce)*

*Wendover Marauder another fine winning dog from the world famous Kennels of Mr. and Mrs. L. C. James. (Photo: Diane Pearce)*

*Chestnut of Welbeck bred by Mr./Mrs. R. S. Burns. (Photo: Diane Pearce)*

*Sh. Ch. Stephenshill Gamebird bred by Mr. N. W. Morrish. (Photo: Diane Pearce)*

*An excellent profile is shown by Sh. Ch. Wendover Lady May. The Wendover Kennels owned by Mr./Mrs. L. C. James have produced a long line of champions and are fine examples of carefully planned breeding.*